PRIVATE EYE

Colemanballs
6

A selection of quotes,
most of which originally appeared
in PRIVATE EYE's
'Colemanballs' column.
Our thanks once again
to the readers who
sent us their
contributions.

COLEMANBALLS TOP TEN

PLACE	NAME	ENTRIES
1	DAVID COLEMAN	77
2	MURRAY WALKER	54
3	SIMON BATES	46
4	TED LOWE	34
5	RON PICKERING	27
6	PETER JONES	23
7	HARRY CARPENTER	22
8	BRIAN MOORE	21
9	BRYON BUTLER	15
10	TREVOR BAILEY	14

COMPOSITE TOTAL FIGURES COMPILED BY THE NEASDEN INSTITUTE OF STATISTICS, E&OE

PRIVATE EYE
Colemanballs
6

Compiled and edited by
BARRY FANTONI

Illustrated by Larry

PRIVATE EYE · CORGI

Published in Great Britain
by Private Eye Productions Ltd,
6 Carlisle Street, London W1V 5RG,
in association with Corgi Books

© 1992 Pressdram Ltd
ISBN 0 552 13996 3

Designed by Bridget Tisdall
Printed in Great Britain by
Cox & Wyman Ltd, Reading

Corgi Books are published by Transworld Publishers Ltd,
61–63 Uxbridge Road, Ealing, London W5 5SA,
in Australia by Transworld Publishers (Australia) Pty. Ltd,
15–23 Helles Avenue, Moorebank, NSW 2170
and in New Zealand by Transworld Publishers (N.Z.) Ltd,
3 William Pickering Drive, Albany, Auckland

Athletics

Q: "How do you feel, Kris?"
A: "I just want to keep my feet on the ground."
KRIS AKABUSI

"...and this after three false starts – well, two false starts and one faulty start..."
DAVID COLEMAN

"Kirsty Wade has found a suitable position, at the back of the field."

DAVID COLEMAN

"And now a look at the leaders table: and the good news is that it's all European – Ericsson of Sweden, followed by Westley of Canada."

RON PICKERING

"Four hundred metre running – in terms of its depth reaching new peaks."

DAVID COLEMAN

"Coming up to the finishing line now, with 400 metres to go!"

DAVID COLEMAN

"And if he goes clear at this height, he'll really take the competition by the scruff of the throat."
RON PICKERING

"He wasn't checking who was behind him – he was just looking who it was."
BRENDAN FOSTER

"She's as safe as an olive."
DAVID COLEMAN

"Are there any more great swimmers in the pipeline?"
CLIFF MORGAN

"She's really tough; she's remorseful."
DAVID MOORCROFT

"That race was all about competition."
DAVID COLEMAN

"There's nothing athletes like – or indeed hate –
more than hanging around like this."
DAVID COLEMAN

"Kiptanui, the 19-year-old, turned 20 a few weeks
ago."
DAVID COLEMAN

"She [Jennifer Stout] is looking up at the replay
which she's ignoring."
DAVID COLEMAN

"Absolutely right, but just a fraction wrong."
DAVID COLEMAN

"She is running above herself."
BRENDAN FOSTER

"There's no doubt at all that Liz McColgan has split the Ethiopian completely."

DAVID COLEMAN

"...the almost unknown Kenyan came here with a big reputation."

DAVID COLEMAN

"They are still faster – although their times are the same."

DAVID COLEMAN

"There's only three thousand people here tonight, and they're making enough noise for four thousand."

HARRY CARPENTER

"All the running will be in his legs by the time he gets there."

BRENDAN FOSTER

Bowls

"David [Bryant] was giving 101% in effort which is the least you can ask..."

TONY ALLCOCK

Boxing

"Well, there it is – the judges have given a draw, but we'll be back in a couple of minutes to talk to the loser."

REG GUTTRIDGE

"I want to be able to walk the streets of London anywhere in the world."

LLOYD HONEYGHAN

"I was 18 about six years ago – I'm 28 now."

FRANK BRUNO

"It's a no win or lose situation."

GLENN McCRORY

"I think if he knocked the man out cold, the referee would have to step in and stop it."

JIM WATT

"He's got a little notch in his brain which he turns off."

FRANK BRUNO

"I don't want to look further than as far as I can see."

FRANK BRUNO

"I was in a no-win situation, so I'm glad I won rather than lost."

FRANK BRUNO

"Sure, there've been deaths and injuries in boxing, but none of them serious."

ALAN MINTER

"It's a clash of styles. Martin's a plodder, Gary's a plodder..."

ALAN MINTER

INTERVIEWER: "So, how far do you think you can go in boxing?"
BOXER: "Well, I've been to Africa."

MANCHESTER PICCADILLY RADIO

"And then he [Tyson] will have only channel vision."

FRANK BRUNO

Cricket

"He didn't drop the bat. It fell out of his hand."

RAY ILLINGWORTH

"Top scorer so far is Watkinson with his 50 or Atherton with his 40."

BRIAN JOHNSTON

"In many ways this is Allan Lamb."

TOM GRAVENEY

"...and Dickie Bird standing there with his neck between his shoulders."

BRIAN JOHNSTON

"If Gower had stopped that, it would have decapitated his hand."

FAROKH ENGINEER

"The replay, which the umpire doesn't have the benefit of, shows that he was either an inch in or an inch out."

RICHIE BENAUD

"He stood on tiptoe, on the back foot and drove the ball on the off. I don't know how you'd describe that shot."

RAY ILLINGWORTH

"And in their second game of the season, Lancashire have at last notched up a victory."

COMMENTATOR

"I'm not one to blame anyone, but it was definitely Viv Richards' fault."

FRED TRUEMAN

"Malcolm Marshall scored a handful of runs at Headingley... nought and one."

JACK BANNISTER

"That's another nail in what looks like being a very good score."

JACK BANNISTER

"And I can see the strong wind blowing the sun towards us."

BRIAN JOHNSTON

The sign reads: SAVE THE STEEPLE FUND

"A church spire nestling among the trees... there's probably a church there too."

RICHIE BENAUD

"I won't say it's easier, but it's easier."

RAY ILLINGWORTH

"England have their noses in front – not only actually but metaphorically too."

TONY COZIER

"A couple of the Indian fielders now are streaming
out very slowly."

S. GAVASKAR

"His absence can never quite be replaced here at
Lords."

HENRY BLOFELD

"Kapil Dev seems to have a preconceived idea in
his head, but he doesn't know what it is."

TONY LEWIS

"Well, I shall remember that catch for many a
dying day."

BRIAN JOHNSTON

"There must be something on Gooch's mind, and he wants to get it off his chest."

FAROKH ENGINEER

"West Indies have got to dig deep to get out of this hole they're in."

COMMENTATOR

"There were no heroes out there; they were all heroes!"

CHRIS TURNER

"He used to work for a very well-known firm, can't remember who they are..."

BRIAN JOHNSTON

Cycling

"Andre Vandapole has four silver medals in cyclocross, and none of them gold."

PHIL LIGGOT, CHANNEL 4

Football

"Football today would certainly not be the same if it had never existed."

ELTON WELSBY

"Those are the sort of doors that get opened if you don't close them."

TERRY VENABLES

"Before the game our dressing room was like Dunkirk before they went over the trenches."

JOHN SILLET

"England have just scored their second goal from a penalty corner. This will add to their first goal."

RON JONES

"And again the game's turned round on its head."

TREVOR BROOKING

"Oh, that's good running on the run."

JOHN MOTSON

"It's a football stadium in the truest sense of the word."

JOHN MOTSON

"He put his body between himself and the defender."

PAUL STURROCK

"He has always played for Inter Milan, whilst his brother plays just across the city at AC Milan, who of course share the same stadium."

BRIAN MOORE

"...and Brian Clough, looking suitably chaste..."

ALAN PARRY

"I never predict anything and I never will do."

PAUL GASCOIGNE

"George [Graham] will be happy with a draw – I know how ambitious and positive he is."

TERRY NEILL

"When you think about it, there's three games per working week – Saturday, mid-week and Saturday again."

JIMMY GREAVES

"Gary Lineker – trying to get that hamstring to the ball!"

TREVOR BROOKING

"It was a bit like a game of chess; they kicked the ball from one end to the other."

JOHN MONIE

"Dave Cooper – the spark they hope will unlock this formation."

GERRY HARRISON

"Gullit... turned to find he had someone standing on his toes."

JOHN MOTSON

"It's a good job I'm not colour blind because both teams are playing in black and white."

HARRY GRATION

"There's one that hasn't been cancelled because of the Arctic conditions – it's been cancelled because of a frozen pitch."

BOB WILSON

"It's as if there's a laser beam in his chest attracting the ball."

JIMMY HILL

"...and tonight we have the added ingredient of Kenny Dalglish not being here."

MARTIN TYLER

"And 1st division Luton have haunted themselves with their own play."

TONY GUBBA

"I wonder whether Man United are missing the absence of Bruce?"

TREVOR FRANCIS

"He's captain of Rangers and that's one of the reasons he's captain."

WALTER SMITH

"Without picking out anyone in particular, I thought Mark Wright was tremendous."

GRAEME SOUNESS

"I've nothing to prove: I've got to prove to Southampton I can still score goals."

ALAN SHEARER

"As the ball came over, Speed threw his head at it."

COMMENTATOR

"If it comes to penalties – one of these two great sides could go out on the whim of a ball."

PETER SHREEVE

"And Lineker scored the equaliser thirteen minutes before the end – talk about a last-minute goal!"

SIMON MAYO

"They compare him to Steve Heighway and he's nothing like him, but I can see why – it's because he's a bit different."

KEVIN KEEGAN

"You cannot guarantee a thing in this game. All you can guarantee is disappointment."

GRAEME SOUNESS

"It's the original David against Goliath here."
COMMENTATOR

"Nichol never gives more than 120%."
KEVIN KEEGAN

"John Brown was on the dole two years ago
working as a baker in Inverness."
COMMENTATOR

"Chris Waddle is off the field at the moment;
exactly the position he is at his most menacing."
GERALD SINSTAD

"Fortunately, there's no surface water lying on top of the pitch."

JIMMY ARMFIELD

"I know we had home advantage, which does give you an advantage. But nothing to be feared, though."

BOBBY ROBSON

"The crowd not surprisingly standing on their feet."

TREVOR BROOKING

"If you never concede a goal, you're going to win more games than you lose."

BOBBY MOORE

"Mark Hughes, Sparky by name and sparky by nature and the same can be said of Steve McMahon."

BRIAN MOORE

"He's looking around at himself."

JIMMY GREAVES

"Perry Groves scoring that Arsenal goal three minutes before the first half."

MIKE INGHAM

"Not being in the Rumbelows Cup for those teams won't mean a row of beans, 'cos that's only small potatoes."

IAN ST JOHN

"Oldham are leading 1-0, a well-deserved victory at this stage of the game."

TOMMY DOCHERTY

"As I've said before and I've said in the past..."
KENNY DALGLISH

"There is no way Ryan Giggs is another George Best. He is another Ryan Giggs."

DENIS LAW

"...and Tranmere Rovers are playing with a 5-man back four."

COMMENTATOR

"There's no job in football I've ever wanted. This is the only job in football I've ever wanted."

KEVIN KEEGAN

"This must be Football's busiest mid-week night of the season..."

BOB HALL

"For those of you who know the Selhurst Park Ground, West Ham are playing from right to left."
COMMENTATOR

"Sammy McIlroy – a great player, both on and off the field."

PETER JONES

"It's been a night of frustration. United can't find an end to the cul-de-sac."

ALAN PARRY

"The day is coming when Rangers will be looking over their shoulder and wondering how we [Celtic FC] got so far ahead."

TERRY CASSIDY

"Aberdeen are taking this bitter pill on the chin."
COMMENTATOR

"At times he gave us what Barnes and Waddle could have given us but couldn't because they didn't play."

BOBBY ROBSON

"And so it's West Ham one, Everton nil – and that's the way it stayed all through half-time."

MICK LOWES

"In goalkeeping terms, Chris Turner is 5ft 11in."

RON JONES

"Ablett – wringing his head with disappointment..."

JIMMY GREAVES

"If you [Ian St John] had stopped being the player you were, you wouldn't have been the player you've been."

BOBBY CAMPBELL

"We kept ourselves going because we believed the corner would turn."

DAVE BASSETT

"Some of the football Chelsea have played this afternoon is synonymous with some of the football Chelsea can play."

CAPITAL GOLD REPORTER

World Cup Special

"England under siege now, perhaps for the first time in a length of time."

JOHN MOTSON

"He is without doubt the greatest sweeper in the world, I'd say, at a guess."

RON ATKINSON

"This night of disappointment has been brought to you by ITV and National Power."

BRIAN MOORE

INTERVIEWER: "Did you underestimate them?"
BOBBY ROBSON: "No... but they played better than we thought."

ENGLAND V CAMEROON

"There are two ways of getting the ball – one way is from your own players, and that's the only way."

TERRY VENABLES

"That ball was glued to his right foot, all the way to the back of the net."

ALAN PARRY

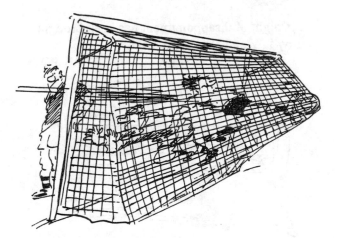

"He [Van Basten] was lucky to not avoid getting sent off."

TREVOR FRANCIS

BRIAN MOORE: "...the whistle's gone, Ray Houghton clearly 4 or 5 yards offside..."
RON ATKINSON: "Yes, but for me that's when Houghton is at his most dangerous."

ENGLAND V EIRE

"Platt... singularly in two minds."

JOHN MOTSON

"Hodge has been unfit for two weeks – well, no, for fourteen days."

BOBBY ROBSON

"We're going to Wembley. We're going to Wembley."

SUPPORTERS, ENGLAND V CAMEROON

"We've got to win tonight, or we've not got to lose. So really we're playing for two results."

BOBBY ROBSON

"Let's close our eyes and see what happens."
                                    JIMMY GREAVES

"It may have just been going wide, but
nevertheless it was a great shot on target."
                                    TERRY VENABLES

"An equalizer here, remember, could lead to a
level score after 90 minutes."
                                    ELTON WELSBY

"...the two supporters of both teams..."
                                    COLIN MOYNIHAN

"Haji has been probably the best player on the field without any question."

BOBBY CHARLTON

"Czechoslovakia ahead a goal to nil – that's a win if it stays that way."

COMMENTATOR

"A semi-final is, as we all know, a semi-final – it's the old cliché."

TERRY NEILL

"There's no such thing as an easier route, but it's an easier route."

BOBBY ROBSON

"And they've visibly grown in stature – even the 5ft 6in Ramirez."

ALAN PARRY

"Your subject is the football World Cup. It's not just football and it's not just the World Cup. It's the football World Cup."

HENRY KELLY

"At 34 nobody will feel the heat more than him."
COMMENTATOR

"All the Argentineans swarmed around him – most of all Maradona."
BRIAN MOORE

"Because there is such a big difference in times, the matches will be recorded and shown either before or afterwards."
IAN FISHER

Golf

"And no one's ever won The Open three times. It's been won four times and two times, but never in its history has it been won three times."
U.S. GOLF COMMENTARY

"I am learning not to get too excited after one good round and to keep my head on the ground."
COLIN MONTGOMERY

"The temperature has shot up a little bit."

PETER ALLIS

"Nick Faldo this afternoon is all in blue, with a white shirt."

TONY ADAMSON

"That will go down in my memory banks for as long as I can remember."

IAN BAKER-FINCH

"There's Clive Clarke moving swiftly across the fairway, like a statue."

PETER ALLIS

Gulf War

"The Iraqi Foreign Minister has said a war in the Gulf won't be like a Rambo film – it will be bloody, long and terrible."

BBC RADIO 5

"The length of the war depends on how long it might be."

JONATHAN DIMBLEBY

"The pilots described it as a turkey shoot because the Iraqis were sitting ducks."

NEWS PRESENTER

"I'm not saying that the Ministry of Defence in London does not have the whole picture of what is going on, but they only have a partial one."

SIR DAVID STEEL

"This is not a news blackout; I just can't tell you anything."

AIR FORCE SPOKESMAN

"23 Japanese tourists have crossed over the Iraqi border into Jordan. They are believed to be the first Westerners to be released from Iraq."

RADIO 4 NEWS

"Saddam Hussein may still have Scud missiles up his sleeve. That could be his last throw of the dice further down the road."

GRAMPIAN TV

"Is there not a cosmetic carrot that could save this man's [Saddam Hussein's] bacon?"

MIKE MORRIS

"It was unexpected because it happened at a time when we didn't think it would."

BRITISH COMMANDER

"This is an unprecedented incident, but we do know it has happened before."

BRIG-GEN PAT FOOTE

"And today will go down in history as January 17 1991."

CLASSIC GOLD RADIO

"A bogus sham!"

JOHN MAJOR

"That was a strategic target, which I prefer to call a strategic target."

VICE-ADMIRAL LAUTENBACHER

"Who he [Saddam Hussein] kills dies."

JEFFREY ARCHER

"We seem to have unleashed a hornets' nest."

VALERIE SINGLETON

Horses

"If I hadn't already won three Nationals, I'd think I was fated never to win it."

TIM FORSTER

"Let's hope he starts riding winners like a machine gun."

JOHN OAKSEY

"Their [the horses'] tendons are like elastic, if they stretch them, they don't go back together again."

IRISH HORSE TRAINER

"There's Alan Munro. He's easy to spot because he's difficult to spot, if you pardon the pun."
JOHN FRANCOME

"She's got a heart as big as iron."
JOHN FRANCOME

"Northern trainers have got a lot of ammunition in their larder."
RICHARD PITMAN

"Marling – unbeaten in her three victories."
PETER O'SULLIVAN

"He looked like a cat on a hot brick roof."
JOHN FRANCOME

Literally

"You can row down the river, literally, following in Constable's footsteps."

'TRAVEL SHOW', BBC

"Mike Pigg, known affectionately as 'Piglet' – literally eating up the road behind the bike of Barel."

COMMENTATOR

"He literally carried that horse over the treble."

STEPHEN HADLEY

"I was just one of the boys, literally."

RACHEL HAYHOE-FLINT

"...Our soldiers are literally sitting ducks."

CHILTERN RADIO

"...Archbishop Tutu was literally mobbed to pieces yesterday..."

JON SNOW

Maxwell

TREVOR MACDONALD: "How was Mr Maxwell feeling in the last few days?"
RICHARD STOTT (Mirror editor): "He was in a very buoyant mood."

ITN

"Robert Maxwell was discovered missing..."

PETER SNOW

"It will take a long time for the waters to clear..."

MICHAEL PARKINSON

"Mr Maxwell was last seen walking alive on deck at 4.45 this morning."

TREVOR MACDONALD

"...We do not need another sole proprietor who will bully and steal when we can do it ourselves."

PAUL FOOT

Motor Sport

"The beak of the Ayrton Senna chicken is pushing its way through the shell."

MURRAY WALKER

"Those days of Stirling Moss seem to be gone for ever, and long may they continue."

WILLIAM WOLLARD

"Mansell is almost metaphorically in sight of the chequered flag."

MURRAY WALKER

"You can certainly tell a lot about the mood of a car from its body language."

JAMES HUNT

SCALETRIX
MODEL CAR RACING

"It seems to me as if Senna literally just got his nose under the back end of Nanini's car and shoved him out the way..."

TONY COOK

"He's completely unoverawed by Senna."

JAMES HUNT

"Mansell, Senna, Prost. Put them in any order and you end up with the same three drivers."

DEREK WARWICK

"And the gap, which was just under five seconds, is now just over four."

MURRAY WALKER

"If Alain Prost wants to catch Ayrton Senna, he'll have to get on his bike."

JAMES HUNT

"I can't find the words to explain how mortified whoever was responsible for whatever happened must be."

MURRAY WALKER

"This would have been Senna's third win in a row had he won the two before."

MURRAY WALKER

"Both drivers are fundamentally wearing white helmets."

JAMES HUNT

"We are in lap 19 of lap 19."

MURRAY WALKER

Oddballs

"We've already hunted the grey whale into extinction twice."

ANDREA ARNOLD

"Scotland is obviously a very popular part of England."

BARRY FANTONI

"Have you always been small?"

DEREK THOMPSON

"This replica of the Santa Maria – what does it look like?"

JOHN TIDMARSH

"My seven year old, who is now ten..."

LADY OLGA MAITLAND

"It was so tangible I could almost reach out and touch it."

BISHOP OF BRADFORD

"The shape of the business cycle is such that the shoe is pinching."

DOMINIC HARROD

"We don't appear to have Jim Fish on the line at the moment."

NEWSREADER

"...it's like a door slamming, and indeed it is a door because when that door slams it's curtains."
COMMENTATOR

"Half the population is aged over 40, not under."
LAUREN BACALL

"...the Mermaid Theatre's pantomime is *Treasure Island*, and in the title rôle – Frank Windsor..."
STEVE ALLEN

"Mozart is celebrating the 200th anniversary of his death."

DEREK JAMESON

"The fruits of the labours coming home to roost..."
LADY VICTORIA LEATHAM

"...his brilliant performance in One Claudius."
TERRY WOGAN

"There is no such thing as a surgical strike, as the scalpel can turn into a club and have a boomerang effect."

JEREMY PAXMAN

"This is a tried and practised scheme. It's not a fly in the pan idea."

MIKE MORRISON

"The overall trend we have had over the past year or so has not been continued in the last twelve months."

MICHAEL SHERSBY

"The One Man show you do, is that just you?"

TERRY WOGAN

"If you can sort that out, you're a better man than me."

ANGELA RIPPON

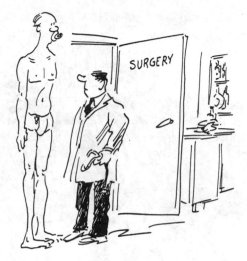

"A child may be, in adult life, quite a tall child."
DOCTOR

"If you think of the other hostages – you take
Terry Waite and Paul McCartney – their families
have behaved impeccably."
SIR JOHN STOKES

"If Michael and Carol haven't got it, it must be
pretty difficult, so if you haven't got it at home,
well done."
RICHARD WHITELY

"I'd like to do a hands up test to find out how many ladies are wearing their thermals today."

EVE POLLARD

"And what really fills me with confidence is that the Class 91 is exceeding all its failure targets early – and is the most reliable locomotive on British Rail."

DAVID ROLLIN

"...so before a storm in a tea-cup brews, nip it in the bud."

RUSSELL GRANT

"With the Euro-Disney World soon to be built just across the Channel, British Theme Parks will just seem Mickey Mouse affairs."

NEIL WALKER

"...and in our next programme we'll be looking at blind dogs for the guide."

SIMON GROOM

"Cardial – as in cardial arrest."

EVE POLLARD

"[The new] Liverpool St Station... the greatest development in London since the Great Fire of 1666."

GUY MICHELMORE

"The flagship of NHS reforms has run aground and is sinking fast."

GUY'S HOSPITAL WORKER

"A small doubt, no bigger than a man's hand, must have crept into your mind."

TERRY WOGAN

"There are all sorts of strings to this offer which still haven't been ironed out."

JOHN FRYER, BBC1

"But these days you go down to B&Q or MFI and buy it ready assembled, you know, you assemble it yourself."

DEREK JAMESON

"Having a baby is one of the hardest and most strenuous things known to man."

ANNA RAEBURN

"A car's a car. I suppose there's some truth in that."

DEREK JAMESON

"They're great ones for facial expressions and sounds with their mouth, the Japanese."

JACK NEWTON

NURSE (explaining scanner treatment): "The treatment comes in three stages."
ROBBIE VINCENT: "Let's get that right – that is stage one, then stage two, then stage three."

BBC1

Politics

"We don't condone the looting and violence. But the police used a water cannon to put out a lighted match and inflamed the situation."

STEVE NALLY

"Sustainable growth is growth that is sustainable."

JOHN MAJOR

"Mrs Thatcher was a wonderful world statesman."

LADY PORTER

"Both economically, politically and socially."

NEIL KINNOCK

"This is the first step in a chain that will unfold."

DAVID MELLOR

"Rajiv Gandhi was not the man his mother was the woman."

SIR ELDON GRIFFITHS

"It's a political hot potato round their necks..."
DR MARKS

"Labour are pushing lies through our doorstep."
WILLIAM WALDEGRAVE

"I will never forget the '81 – or was it '82? –
honours list."

JULIAN CRITCHLEY

"When they (the IRA) plant such bombs, it proves
they can scare people, it proves they can kill
people, it proves nothing."

PETER BOTTOMLEY

"Peter Brooke and Gerry Collins issued a
communiqué condemning the latest lengths to
which the IRA have sunk."

NEWSNIGHT

"The single overwhelming two facts were..."

PADDY ASHDOWN

"He's faced with the eternal European triangle...
which makes it very difficult to square the circle."

JOHN COLE

"We'll be heading for deepening heights of
recession."

LIBERALS' ECONOMIC SPOKESMAN

"So you've finally nailed your mast to Neil Kinnock?"

INTERVIEWER

"We took the kettle off the boil and overheated the economy."

GEOFFREY DICKENS

"What is the use of all these countries sending us aid, and then below the table kicking us in the teeth?"

THAI ECONOMIC SPOKESMAN

"Working mothers are the backbone of the third half of the economy."

GLENDA JACKSON

"Mr Bush is the first living US president to visit Czechoslovakia."

VOICE OF AMERICA

"Michael Heseltine should come out of the woodwork, stop waving his plastic chickens about, run his flag up the flag-pole and see who salutes."

JOHN BANHAM

"There's a lot been made of this dirty man of Europe business, but I don't think it washes."

TOM BURKE

"I think there are many, many people who could replace Margaret Thatcher when she finally hangs up her fighting boots."

NORMAN TEBBIT

"I wish I could have been a fly on the wall inside Mrs Thatcher's brain."

GILL CRONE

"If there is a leadership challenge, it will take place."

KENNETH BAKER

"Her decision was quite decisive."

JOHN COLE

"I hear the stench of appeasement."

MARGARET THATCHER

"There were many highs and lows during their 8 years at the White House – low points like cancer. And perhaps the lowest of all, when President Reagan survived an assassination attempt."

JOHN DUNN

"I went up the greasy pole of politics step by step..."

MICHAEL HESELTINE

"Bringing the leadership to its knees occasionally, is a good way of keeping it on its toes."

TONY BANKS, ITV

"Interlinked but separate."

DAVID OWEN

"It's like a game of chess; all the cards are thrown in the air, the board's turned over and you're in a completely new ball game."

ANTHONY HOWARD

"A man was arrested after trying to shoot President Gorbachev in Red Square today. It was not known whether the man was making an assassination attempt."

NEWS HEADLINES

"This is a window of opportunity for us to step in to..."

TOM KING

"You know what they say – don't get mad, get angry."

EDWINA CURRIE

"They [local authorities] are caught between the deep blue sea of the rates and the frying-pan of the Poll Tax."

TORY BACKBENCHER

"The faintest of rumours, no larger than a man's hand..."

JOHN SIMPSON

"If the Islamic revolution doesn't deliver you food, you've got egg all over your face."

JONATHAN DIMBLEBY

"The Labour Party want to destroy the bottom rung of the escalator."

MICHAEL HOWARD

Pop

"The Wiz is based on The Wizard of Oz. It's like a musical version of it."

> SINITTA

"I ran into Billy Idol at a soirée this morning."
> STEVE WRIGHT

"The temperature is gradually plunging."
> TONY BLACKBURN

"Later we have the winning competition prizewinners."

> MARK GOODIER

"We've been old friends for a long time."
> CHRIS LOWE

"Letter-writing isn't everyone's strongest forte."
> SIMON BATES

"I shouldn't be eating with my mouth full."
JASON DONOVAN

"My ambition for 1991 was to see Robert Ward play on a British stage. This I fulfilled, but I had to go to Holland to do it."

ANDY KERSHAW

"It's been a real gravy train for a long time; now the gravy has come home to roost on the shirt."
ROBBIE VINCENT

"He woke up in the morning with a headache like an elephant had been sitting on his chest all night."

SIMON BATES

"This guy's a legend. He goes back to the time when er... I guess, your parents were your grandparents."

SIMON BATES

"The music sums up the series better than the series does..."

SIMON BATES

"Of course, he [John Lennon] would have been a survivor too had he lived."

PATRICIA HAYES

"That was the inimitable Edith Piaf. Can anybody else sing like her?"

NIGEL DEMPSTER

"They were twins... well, they were born a 3/4 hour apart, so not really twins."

SIMON BATES

"Your ambition, is that right – to abseil across the Channel?"

CILLA BLACK

"Some songs were released one year and in the charts the next, and vice versa."

MIKE REID

"Short of a major scandal, that band [Huey Lewis & The News] will continue to make records and entertain people for the next 25 years, as will this next artist, the late Jim Croce."

DAVE LEE TRAVIS

"We have really opened a worm's nest..."

SIMON BATES

"They've pinpointed a date for the concert – it's
sometime between June and September..."

SIMON BATES

"We're both agreed – we'll do the programme
from Bogota, Columbia, when New Kids are on
the Block there..."

SIMON BATES

"So nip up to the loft and check out your old
singles to see if there are any that were played a lot
on the radio, but you never got round to buying."

GARY KING

"Rachel... hello, what's your name?"

PHILIP SCHOFIELD

"Of course he [Jim Morrison] is dead now, which
is a high price to pay for immortality."

GLORIA ESTEFAN

"Faith, Hope and Charity,
Love is the greatest of the three."

FRANCES NERO

"You can be famous or infamous. I think we're a bit of both."

MATT GOSS

"The 16th Century four-poster bed was originally owned by Mick Jagger and Marianne Faithfull."

TOMMY PUETT

"This track is brilliant. I played it for the first time last week and we are doing the same this week."

PHILIP SCHOFIELD

"I like dolphins. If dolphins were human, I'd be a dolphin."

JASON DONOVAN

"In fact, the music in 'Children of Eden' is not as bad as it sounds."

SHERIDAN MORLEY

Questions & Answers

CALLER: "Hello, Doug, I'm a single mother."
DOUGLAS CAMERON: "Oh, and have you got any children?"

LBC

CALLER: "My name is actually Nellie."
GARY DAVIES: "Why?"
CALLER: "Because it's my name."

RADIO 1

MARK CURRY: "What are you doing this morning?"
CALLER: "Listening to the radio."

BBC PHONE-IN

PHIL UPTON: "When are you 18?"
CALLER: "Next Tuesday".
UPTON: "So that's your birthday?"

BRMB RADIO

INTERVIEWER: "So you are the camp co-ordinator. What does that entail?"
VENTURE SCOUT: "Well, basically, I co-ordinate the camp."

'8.15 FROM MANCHESTER'

SIMON BATES: "And, strangely enough, this air traffic control room has no windows."
RAF PERSON: "Well, actually it's the radar room."
SIMON BATES: "So how do you manage to see the planes?"
RAF PERSON: "By radar."

RADIO 1

SIMON BATES: "You say that your first language was Gaelic. Do you mean that Gaelic was the language you spoke before you learned to speak English?"
INTERVIEWEE: "Yes."

SIMON BATES: "So what do you do?"
SOLDIER: "I'm an electrician."
SIMON BATES: "So what's that in layman's terms?"

MARK GOODIER: "What's the name of the company you work for?"
LISTENER: "Mining and Engineering Services."
MARK GOODIER: "So, what kind of work do they do: is it mining and engineering services?"

GARY DAVIES: "And what do you do for a living?"
LISTENER: "I'm a freelance writer."
DAVIES: "Really? Who do you work for?"
LISTENER: "Er... myself."

GARY DAVIES: "What kind of box was it?"
WOMAN: "It was a guitar case."
GARY DAVIES: "What was in it?"
WOMAN: "A guitar."

RADIO 1

BRUCE FORSYTH: "Have you got any kids?"
CONTESTANT: "A daughter of 4, and twins,
David and Samantha, who are 1."
BRUCE FORSYTH: "Twins! How lovely. What are
they – a boy and a girl?"

BBC1

LES DENNIS: "And you're a music teacher, aren't
you, Paul?"
CONTESTANT: "Yes, that's right, from
Derbyshire."
LES DENNIS: "And what do you teach?"
CONTESTANT: "Er... music."

CENTRAL ITV

DAVE LEE TRAVIS: "So, where are you from?"
LISTENER: "York, Dave."
DLT: "Aaah, York in... er..."
LISTENER: "Yorkshire, Dave."

RADIO 1

POLICEMAN: "Do you speak German? Or French?"
LORRY DRIVER: "Only Czech."
POLICEMAN: "Driving here is verboten."

'FIRST TUESDAY'

GUEST: "My company makes kitchen tiles."
ANDREW O'CONNOR: "And what type of kitchen tiles are they?"
GUEST: "They are the type you would expect to find in your kitchen."

BBC1

SHANE RITCHIE: "Where did you shoot your video?"
CONTESTANT: "Ibiza."
SHANE RITCHIE: "Have you been to Ibiza?"

BBC1

JEANNE DOWNS: "So has Britain broken any records recently?"
NORRIS MCWHIRTER: "Well, everyone in Britain on Friday took part in Britain's hottest day yet."
PRESENTER: "So, is that a world record then?"
NORRIS : "Er, no, it's a British record."

CHILDREN'S ITV

JIMMY HILL: "Don't sit on the fence Terry, what chance do you think Germany have of getting through?"

TERRY VENABLES: "I think it's fifty-fifty."

BBC1

EMMA FREUD: "You knew Ludovic Kennedy when he was three. What was he like as a three-year-old?"

VISCOUNT WHITELAW: "Well, he was a three-year-old."

BBC2

JIM BOWEN: "You're a fisherman, aren't you?"

CONTESTANT: "That's right, Jim."

JIM BOWEN: "What do you fish for?"

CONTESTANT: "Fish, Jim."

BULLSEYE

JIMMY HILL: "But you said it should have been a goal."

TERRY VENABLES: "No, I didn't. I said it should have been a goal."

JIMMY HILL: "So you've changed your tune then."

BBC1

Rowing

"Britain's first ever women's medal in the World Rowing Championships – yes, it's been a long time out in the desert for our women rowers."

CHRIS BAILLIEU

Rugby

"He hangs his head – looks to the sky..."

NIGEL STARMER-SMITH

"Scott Gibbs, the nineteen year old, now twenty."

BILL MCLAREN

"The Welsh have never had to taste defeat at the hands of the wooden spoon."

PAUL COONEY

"There's no excuse for pace."

ALEX MURPHY

"It takes two teams to make a final – and Widnes have done just that."

RAY FRENCH

"We've got some good players and so have they –
that's the difference."

AUSTRALIAN RUGBY OFFICIAL

"A scrum to Ireland, who have their tails up right
under the Welsh crossbar."

RADIO 5

"Remember, it's a cup final; there won't be any
friends given or taken."

ALEX MURPHY

"We've said it once, we've said it many times,
there's no excuse for pace."

ALEX MURPHY

"...and Shaun Edwards – happy memories of
Wembley; on his last appearance here he received
a fractured cheek-bone."

RAY FRENCH

"Mind you, 39 is a nice round number."

CLIFF MORGAN

"And St Helens have really got their tails between their teeth."

MALCOLM LORD

"You've never been in front in any of the matches you've played, but you've always come out the winners."

ALEX MURPHY

"Twenty-nil; a fairly comfortable lead."

IAN ANDERSON

"A fairy dream come true."

BILL BEAUMONT

"Welsh winger has the ball but Brendan Mullin is breathing down his throat."

HECTOR MACNEILL

Snooker

"It was a game of three halves."

STEVE DAVIS

"Ninety-nine times out of a thousand he would have potted that ball."

COMMENTATOR, POT BLACK

"Going through Jimmy White's mind at the moment will be the winning post."

JOHN PULLMAN

"He's lost ten frames now, and if he loses another it'll be eleven."

DAVID ICKE

"Those memories of that final are now just memories."

JOHN VIRGO

"You've got to have self-confidence in yourself."
STEPHEN HENDRY

"...and I noticed that Jimmy shot out of his chair like a bolt out of a gun."
TED LOWE

"All pots seem alike – the pockets must look like dustbin lids."
JOHN VIRGO

"Tony Meo is eyeing up a plant."
DAVID VINE

Tennis

"Kratzmann is now letting Chang play his own game – and he does that better than anyone."

CHRISTINE JAMES

"And Lendl's been in the semi-finals every year since, except for the two years he was in the final."

JOHN BARRETT

"So I don't think there'll be much Wimbledon going on today – certainly not here up North where it's bucketing down."

CHRIS BELL

"Even when he has to move back, he moves back so that he's moving forwards!"

MARK COX

INTERVIEWER: "So, Pam, what are your interests outside tennis?"
PAM SHRIVER: "Well, I run a tennis school..."

RADIO 2

"And there's Ken Rosewall sitting in the crowd...
what a champion he was... four times runner-up
here at Wimbledon."

BILL THRELFALL

"Zina's come up from the public parks, where
most of the grass roots players start from."

BILLIE-JEAN KING

"The whole depth of talent in World Table Tennis
has never been higher."

PETER WALKER